W9-ALM-805

A Trip to the Pumpkin Patch

BY JENNA LEE GLEISNER

Published by The Child's World®
1980 Lookout Drive • Mankato, MN 56003-1705
800-599-READ • www.childsworld.com

Photographs ©: Romiana Lee/Shutterstock
Images, cover, 1; IS_ImageSource/iStockphoto, 5;
PhotographyPerspectives/iStockphoto, 6; Andy Dean
Photography/Shutterstock Images, 9; Monkey Business
Images/iStockphoto, 10–11; Agnieszka Kirinicjanow/
iStockphoto, 12; Arvind Balaraman/Shutterstock
Images, 15; Christopher Brown/iStockphoto, 17;
Blend Images/Shutterstock Images, 18–19, 20;
Heike Brauer/Shutterstock Images, 22

Design Element: Shutterstock Images

ISBN 9781503816640
LCCN 2016945642

Printed in the United States of America
PA02323

ABOUT THE AUTHOR
Jenna Lee Gleisner is an author
and editor from Minnesota. Her
favorite thing about fall is the
changing colors.

Contents

Picking A Pumpkin

It is a fall day. It is time to visit a pumpkin patch!

4

There are **rows** of pumpkins. Some pumpkins are big. Some are small.

People pick out pumpkins.
One girl picks a **round**
pumpkin.

Pumpkin Patch Fun

There is a **contest**.
Who has the biggest pumpkin?

There is face painting.
Some kids get orange
pumpkins on their cheeks.

There is a hayride.
A **tractor** pulls the wagon
around the patch.

Pumpkin Patch Treats

Some people buy treats. They can buy pumpkin bread.

People take their pumpkins home. They carve them.

19

They **decorate** for Halloween. They set out **jack-o'-lanterns**.

Paint a Pumpkin

You can paint your own pumpkin!

Supplies:

pumpkin   newspaper
black paint   pencil
paintbrush

Instructions:

1. Set your pumpkin on the newspaper.

2. Draw a face on your pumpkin with your pencil. It can be silly or spooky!

3. Dip your paintbrush in the paint.

4. Use your paintbrush to paint over the lines.

5. Let your pumpkin dry.

Glossary

contest — (KAHN-test) A contest is an event where people try to win something. The person with the biggest pumpkin won the contest.

decorate — (DEK-uh-rate) To decorate is to add color or a design. We decorate for Halloween with pumpkins.

jack-o'-lanterns — (JAK-uh-LAN-turnz) Jack-o'-lanterns are pumpkins with faces carved in them. We carved jack-o'-lanterns.

round — (ROWND) Something round is shaped like a circle. I picked a round pumpkin.

rows — (ROHZ) Rows are things set up in a straight line. There were rows of pumpkins.

tractor — (TRAK-tur) A tractor is a vehicle that pulls heavy things. The tractor pulled the hay wagon.

23

To Learn More

Books

Griswold, Cliff. *The Pumpkin Patch.*
New York, NY: Gareth Stevens
Publishing, 2015.

Lee, Jackie. *Pumpkin.* New York, NY:
Bearport Publishing Company, 2016.

Web Sites

Visit our Web site for links about
pumpkins: **childsworld.com/links**

Note to Parents, Teachers, and Librarians: We routinely verify
our Web links to make sure they are safe and active sites. So
encourage your readers to check them out!

Index